Daphne Ellis

D1365496

DANCING AMONG SNAKES

Extra MILE Innovators
Kingston, Jamaica, W.I.
www.extramileja.com

First printed: April 2022

Published by:
Extra MILE Innovators
4 Rochester Avenue, Kingston 8.
Kingston 10, Jamaica W.I.
www.extramileja.com

Cover Design: VividConcepts |vividconcepts@gmail.com
Formatting: BambuSparks | www.bambusparks.com

Author Contact: For consultation, feedback or speaking engagements, contact the author at missdaphneellis@hotmail.com.

To my mother,
who at the time of writing is 97 years old and has
modeled for me, in many different ways, that life's
battles do not have to destroy you.

Praise for *Dancing Among Snakes*

For a first-time author Ms. Ellis' book has the marks of a seasoned writer. Her book Dancing Among Snakes from its beautiful cover design through its arresting real-life narrative, hooks your literary neck, pulls you in and you will not want to be released until she is through delighting, tantalizing, encouraging and challenging you. I have no gift of prophecy, but I suspect this will be a best-seller. Warmest congratulations Ms. Ellis!

Rev. Clinton Chisholm, D.D
Christian Apologist and Author

The author of this frankly exciting book is a Jamaican educator and counselor. Because of her mathematical skills, you can expect to find that everything adds up; learning of life is multiplied, and if you read from cover to cover, your anxiety will be subtracted. She is the proud graduate of two prestigious institutions in Kingston which followed her teacher training. This notwithstanding, a

humbler human being you cannot find. It comes as no surprise, then, that she writes with uncommon enthusiasm, after all, she represents Jahmekyah! (Jamaica), and "arithmetical" precision. But none of the above overrides the Christian conviction with which she expresses herself in this first book.

The reader can expect to be challenged--in one way or the other--to reflect just a little more deeply on life at various levels and more so in the wretched era of the rampant teenager dubbed COVID-19. But not even covid will rob you of the blessing of this book that multiplies positive emotions and takes away that which is pathological. Written by one who believes that principle is Principal, it is especially recommended for people like me, lacking in emotional intelligence. You will ignore this book at your own peril!

Delano Vincent Palmer, ThD

Former Deputy President, JTS

New Testament Scholar

Daphne's life experiences have been written with a refreshing honesty that fully engages her reader. Her prose delivers intriguing depth in expressive clarity to share her story. This is an account that details just how one overcomes in the face of intense adversity.

A rare gem of a book, you will find yourself unable to put this riveting page-turner down as you journey with her to personal growth at its best. Along the way you will laugh, cry, and feel a range of emotions as you navigate familiar and new territory, making your way to a triumphant end. Daphne will show you that you too, can dance, even in the most challenging times as you learn to lean on God- the one who she clearly allowed to chart her path and choreograph her movements to victory.'

Dianne Chambers

Educator and Fine Artist

What a gem from this first-time author! From the very first paragraph it grabs you and takes you on a roller coaster ride through uncharted territories, while sprinkling valuable nuggets of life-lessons along the way! Wow! I intended to "spot-through" this manuscript, as I usually do, then, after getting to know the author's style and direction, come back to digest it in its entirety and depth.

Not so! I must admit I was forced to go through it, chapter by chapter, to be sure that I didn't miss any of its words of wisdom, which if followed, can make life a great deal easier and much more enjoyable. Can't wait to try out some of these principles! I enjoyed this read a lot! Can't wait for her next offering!

Othneil Brown

Author and Pharmaceutical Manager

Introduction

As I share my experiences at different seasons of my life and from various spaces, I am conscious of how challenging this journey can be. I am deeply aware that despite how low we may feel, there is a power to prevail that lies inside each of us, even though we may not want to believe it. Sometimes we do not think we can carry on, but there are persons and experiences that can serve as a buffer, and a source of hope and encouragement, so we rise to fight again. *Dancing Among Snakes* affirms that there is hope and we can have testimonies of victory despite life's challenges

In this book, I recall bouts of depression, frustration, and long battles with feelings of anger and bitterness. I know what being let down by trusted friends feels like. I have experienced the emotional upheavals associated with unfair treatment. I have questioned how unfair life can be, and have at times, wondered if I could ever forgive. I faced despair and struggled with regaining trust. At times I felt like I was suspect of everyone who tried to get close to me. But I also know what it feels like to overcome.

As an educator, who has served in different capacities in my homeland Jamaica and overseas, I have experienced some of my fiercest battles in doing what I know I have been called to do. My Christian faith, and support from different persons at different times, helped in strengthening me at some of my weakest and most painful moments. I have named one of my pastoral leaders 'Captain' as he came into my life at a point where my ship would certainly have run aground. I was unsure I would have survived that shipwreck.

The symbol of the snake portrays the pain, the attacks, the misunderstandings, the false accusations and so much more. The dance speaks of victory, and these symbols were born out of a dream I had when it seemed I had reached the peak of my career. Dancing among snakes is a testimony of triumph. It is meant to give hope, to lift the spirit, and say, *you can find the strength to dance again if you do not give up.* This can give the assurance that the psalmist describes with the change that can come after the pain. "You did it: you changed wild lament into whirling dance; You ripped off my black mourning band and decked me with wildflowers. I'm about to burst with song; I can't keep quiet about you. God, my God, I can't thank you enough" (Psalms 30:11-12, MSG).

Contents

The Dream

It has been a few years since I had that unforgettable experience. The image still remains in my mind like a framed snapshot concerning which an initial glance would possibly envelop the bravest in fear. It appeared ominous and spine-chilling and totally devoid of the features of a normal play field, as where there should have been matted, manicured grass, there was a thick, shiny-looking carpet of snakes. This was certainly no place to play, much less to dance, but it was as if every feeling of trepidation was eclipsed by an undeniable aura of celebration as I danced effortlessly over these scary, threatening reptiles. Panic seemed to have taken wings as the raised heads, elongated fangs, and forked tongues of these snakes all seemed non-existent. This could not be happening, as I had a deep-seated fear of simple things like flying roaches and small house lizards. This was not an ordinary experience.

I had gone to bed like any other night, having said my prayers and eventually drifting off to sleep. I remember jumping out of sleep to an almost audible voice that declared, "You are dancing among snakes." I was shaking. I felt a forceful pounding in my chest, as if it was about to burst open. It was as if I was still seeing those reptiles. I relived the dream like a movie. Snakes were everywhere as if they had been dumped from a pit and had slithered into a comfortable spot on the playfield. They did not overlap but lay in an intertwined arrangement. It was as if they mockingly yet silently stated, "We are going nowhere. We are here to stay". They seemed at ease in a habitat that was not theirs.

The remarkable feature in this scene, however, was my response. Just as if I was being carried by unseen hands, I was skipping over all the snakes, daring to step into every space among those silent, squeamish looking reptiles, and not one could touch me. I hopped with confidence. I twirled gleefully. I skipped and was celebratory in every move. I had a feeling of euphoria. There was one detail that did not elude me and this bothered me. I had an audience, and there were smiling faces that I could recognize. I woke up from my dream, and like the biblical account of Joseph in the book of Genesis, I wondered what it meant.

I know when my dreams have value or are significant, as they tend to linger in my mind. They are usually so vivid that if I were an artist, I could paint every detail. For a moment, I seemed to have morphed into the character of Pharaoh in the Bible, seeking an interpretation for the dream in my life. The components lingered, causing a sort of uneasiness, and then like a soothing, calming statement, I uttered with relief, "Remember, you were dancing." That statement became a mantra and one that I stated repeatedly over the next few years.

An article in Frontiers in Psychology in May 2019 stated, "Humans perceive snakes as threatening stimuli, resulting in emotional and behavioral responses ... snakes may evoke fear or disgust ... or even both emotions simultaneously." In some African and eastern tribes, snake dancing forms part of their entertainment or religious rituals. There are also interpretations that have been attributed to dreams about dancing snakes. Amanda Arnold referenced author Lauri Quinn Loewenburg, a professional dream analyst, who says that "Just as you would not ignore coming across a snake in real life, neither should you ignore your snake dreams." This snake dream could not be ignored.

So many fear snakes and wherever they are found would certainly not be where the average person would want to dance. The climax in my dream is that the snakes were subdued, and I was the dancer. To me, it spoke of treachery and deception in one sense, yet victory and vindication in another. It said to me, *beware, be cautious, open your eyes.* I recalled the familiar faces, and it made me uneasy, causing a myriad of questions to race all over my mind. In these aftereffects of this dream, I realized that I also had to make a choice as something began to haunt me.

What of those faces that I had identified? My mind seemed to have now gone into overdrive. How do I react around them? They were in my space! I had to work with them! What guarantee did I have that I would not be set up? Was this a nightmare, or was I being given a message? The questions came with haunting discomfort. There was nothing that I could readily identify that were indications of my dream. But there was a deep-seated feeling that there were tumultuous times ahead.

My life was not devoid of challenges from as far back as I could remember. There were relationship challenges, health challenges, financial challenges, and family challenges, so surely, I could weather this. As I looked back over the various ordeals, I could identify a common thread. I was always fighting back. I was never one to play dead or give up. I realize now that I was dancing all along. God was enabling me to continue to dance through and after the various episodes. Despite the mourning seasons, they had been turned to dancing, and that time and again, I experienced what Psalm 30:11, NLT said, "You have turned my mourning into joyful dancing." This time, however, I sensed it would be different. I perceived surprise, shock, and a premonition that there were some 'I can't believe it' moments that lay ahead.

An examination of the behavior of snakes, no matter how cursory, can be quite revealing. They are unpredictable in their movements, and will slither from one spot to another, snap at and seize any bait in their path in a split second. You cannot readily determine whether or not a snake is venomous unless you have studied them. A venomous snake is to be avoided. There are stories of people who have snakes as pets and those same snakes ended up killing them. The wrap of a snake is known to be fatal, and it takes skill and bravery to try to free its victim. For me, snakes are surely not a man's best friend.

I remember visiting a zoo during one of my holiday breaks from school. Among the animals we were introduced to were snakes. They were described as harmless and the workers demonstrated this by holding them, placing them on their shoulders and positions that showed them harmless. Many of the visitors were brave enough to pose with these reptiles, and it felt almost envious not to experience this prowess. I decided I wanted to try.

The zoo staff helped me to hold the snake and I posed ready for my photo opportunity, when suddenly the snake moved. I did not expect that weight and I thought it would remain still. That slight movement brought to my mind the reality that my deep-seated fear of snakes was not removed. I screamed and let it go and my photographer captured that moment, much to my humor up to this day.

There is a Jamaican proverb that says, "Crab sey 'im nuh trust nuh shadder after dark" (The crab says he does not trust any shadow after dark). The meaning implied is to avoid making assumptions about things that are uncertain. Another interesting spin on this proverb is said in this way, "Crab sey 'im nuh trust nuh shadder after dark, not even 'him brudder-in-law,

Lobster.'" (The crab says he does not trust any shadow after dark, not even his brother-in-law, the lobster.). What he thinks is a shadow of a claw, may be a man's hand out to catch him. Trust no shadow after dark.

The Bible tells us not to put confidence in man (Psa. 118:8, KJV). Our parents have shared statements that were like life mantras about how we should relate to people. All of us can look back at tough moments in our lives. Some we hate to relive. Some have challenged us and we have had to fight back feelings of bitterness. Others had us enduring emotional upheavals from which we have had to heal. Others confess being scarred for life because of some of their experiences. "You are dancing among snakes" seemed to embody all of these. I was sure of one thing. I had danced before, and I was going to dance again.

Yes, I *danced!*

The Promotion

I t was just a mere two months after I started this new job. Work had ended for the day and I was heading to a coworker's classroom when I ran into an active member of the school's governing body and we both paused for a quick exchange. We had not been speaking for long before I pierced the air with spontaneous laughter in response to her question. This one truly came from left field and one I was certainly not prepared for. Like Sarah in the Bible, I laughed at what I considered a downright crazy suggestion. This was an impossibility and more so not a desire I ever contemplated. I was enjoying what I was doing, and nothing was going to change that. In my mind, the current institution with all its newness eclipsed aspects of previous experiences that bothered me. I had also decided that would be the last institution in which I would serve.

Memories of my new move came to mind. I remembered the excitement I felt as I packed and made all the necessary preparations. The flight felt special and I was simply happy. I realized that I was going to meet up with a previous co-worker so I was not feeling like I would be a total stranger. I had relocated to a new school on another Caribbean Island and the circumstances that led me there were wrapped up in the words of my favorite Bible text, He has made everything beautiful in his time (Ecclesiastes 3:11, NIV). I began with no dreams, no visions, just a joy to know that I had the assurance that God had led me to this place. I was also satisfied that the timing of my transition was perfect and that I had successfully and satisfactorily completed my task where I previously served.

Words like PACEs, Goal Cards, Self-Test, Pace-Test, Goal Check Reports almost rendered me confused. These were concepts and structures I had never encountered anywhere else. You see, the delivery of the curriculum was unique and even though I had done training in Miami during the summer, I felt like I had been thrown into a pool and had to learn to swim. I had the teaching and classroom management skills, knowledge base and experience, but had to learn a new approach. The first two months were like learning to walk, and indeed it was in more ways than one. I was traveling a different path and I did not realize where God was leading me.

This chance meeting was clearly not in my wildest thoughts, and what I thought was far-fetched became a reality within the next four months. After an interview with the school's Human Resource Department, I was offered the position of principal for the probationary first year. As with any new position or opportunity, there is the usual excitement and hooray in some circles, but it didn't take me long to realize that there were those with whom I walked and talked who did not accept this change. I was not naïve to this reality because this is a part of everyday experiences in many workspaces. However, I chose to ignore these realities and focus on the task that was ahead. And that was when I had that dream.

The impact of this dream lingered and deep down it did cause me to wonder and even consider some possibilities. I had to make a choice whether to walk around in fear or to entrust my day-to-day actions and activities into the hands of the Lord. I chose the latter. There were many things I could use as a crutch when I was at my weakest. In the days following the letter offering me the position, I spent a lot of time in prayer and asked several of my friends to pray with me about the decision and for wisdom to face the task ahead.

There is one response that stands out in my mind and more so because it came from someone whom I had not asked to pray with me. She sent me a note to say that she had been thinking about me and wanted to just share something with me. It was a note from a devotional, and it ended with this statement: "...So, the word for you today is, 'you're qualified for the job'." That seemed to seal the deal and I adjusted my sails to go into uncharted seas.

In the Bible, there is the account of the wilderness wanderings of the children of Israel in their journey to the Promised land of Canaan. Their leader Joshua was charged with the responsibility of leading the new generation into the promised possession. He received a command, which if obeyed, would be a strategy for success, and this was stated in Joshua 1:9, NKJV.

Have not I commanded you? Be strong and of a good courage;

*Do not be afraid, nor be dismayed: for the Lord
your God is with you wherever you go.*

Adhering to this was crucial in seeking to complete their conquest. This was the verse God used to usher me into the position of Principal and the theme for that school year, 'Be Strong and Courageous,' was coined from the verse. At our staff installation service that year, we belted out the lyrics of a Christian hymn by Linda Lee Johnson, "Be Strong in the Lord."

This became my anthem, at other times my mantra and the reminder that I was leading with the assurance of divine presence. I needed to remain strong and courageous. As I was handed the Lamp of Learning in that ceremony, I knew that I was standing on the cusp of uncertainty but undergirded with faith in the One who I knew had opened that door. I learned quickly not to ever forget the circumstances that led to this new position in which I had found myself.

Our pathways in life sometimes take us to places and positions we never dreamed of. As I navigated my responsibilities each day, this verse and this song caressed my soul and mind. Another support system came from the early morning prayers that we had in the chapel. A little before the start of school, staff members would gather in the chapel to pray and commit to the Lord, our day, our students, and the needs of the school. This became my crutch, one of the musical pieces that helped me to dance.

The journey as leader became unpredictable. Battles raged in various forms, and I could not determine what a day would bring. I sometimes could not wrap my head around some of the things that became issues. But the word of the Lord was always there reminding me to be strong and courageous and that strength could come from no one else but the God who led me. I realized and had to say to myself time and again, "remember you were dancing."

It is necessary to create your modus operandi when taking on new responsibilities. It's like entering a marriage, welcoming a new baby, moving to a new country or starting tertiary studies, you must have resources including people and strategies who will help you. From the outset, I carefully selected who and what would be in my arsenal. I was committed to learning the difference between responding and reacting to people and situations. I knew the value of being civil and professional and to use clear and objective plans and guidelines.

Human interactions can sometimes become a serious battleground, but I knew all too well that a refusal or nonacceptance of my decision does not mean that I am wrong, so I should choose my battles. I did not set out to change people but simply to serve. I allowed established principles and required protocols to buffer the tumultuous situations. I was committed to being consistent, fair and impartial in my operations, and above all to pray, pray and pray again.

There is an Aesop fable about a man, his son, and his donkey on their way to the market. They faced a number of verbal attacks at different points along the journey on how fair or not it was in regard to who should be riding the donkey. The debaters determined at one point that it should be the son. Others said the father, while others said no one should burden the beast. In despair, they tied the legs of the donkey and was carrying it across this bridge, and it fell into the water and drowned. A dear friend of mine has repeatedly referenced this account when dealing with challenging situations, by echoing her famous statement: "The last man who tried to please everybody, him donkey drown." I was not on a course to please everyone.

I will not classify the position I held as the father, the son, or the donkey, but I was sure that what God had birthed in me would not be destroyed. Voices would not confuse me, as there is always something or someone that stands out and gives clarity. I looked at and celebrated the victories I experienced and faced each day with all the strength God had given me.

Yes, I *danced!*

3

Friday the 13th: Omen or Reminder

Every culture has its peculiarities and traditions. In Western civilization, it is believed that when the thirteenth day of any month falls on a Friday, it is an unlucky day. Various associations and meanings have been attached to this number, which had its genesis in Scandinavian mythology. Although not establishing a link to this belief, Friday, September 13, 2019, will forever be etched in my mind. This was the day I had an experience that came close to my dream encounter. Its memory still evokes shock and I often ask myself, "Did this really happen?" I guess the omen of Friday the 13th was true for me in one sense, but I still had a victory dance.

My bedroom leads out to a small back porch, and the bedhead faces the door. On that Friday, I woke up like any other morning, stretching quite lazily and lingering under the covers, deeply wishing I could get a few more hours of sleep. Suddenly, something caught my eye, and this immediately catapulted the craving for more sleep far away from me. On the door, I noticed a long hanging figure. It could not be what I perceived. That idea had to be as remote as the hurricane season of 2050. I sat up quickly. I stared. I was beyond terrified.

"This cannot be," I thought. "Am I dreaming again?" I pondered.

I grabbed my glasses, put them on, sat up straight, and stared spellbound. I was speechless, as hanging from the door was a long, black, shiny snake. Its diamond shaped burnished head was pointed down towards the floor. In my eyes, this was a crime scene where it seemed I was beginning to place a caution tape of fear around it. I quickly shrugged that off. I peered at this shocking phenomenon and took note of every feature of this dark reptile as it was hanging against a white door. More details unfolded with my prolonged stare. There was a knot in its body that was unexplainable and quite odd. I perceived it may have been struggling to detach itself from the door, and in so doing, tied itself up. Another perplexing detail here was that it was fastened between the door frame and the top of the closed door and seemed to have been fastened by just a pinch of its skin. The remainder of the body and tail were hung over, forming an uneven letter U.

This made no sense. For me, there was no logical explanation because after all, snakes surely cannot climb up a door. Further to that, I recalled walking through that door the previous evening and saw nothing. I shuddered to think it may have been lying flat on the top of the door and could have fallen on me. I further contemplated why I didn't see it before falling asleep. There was no reasoning on my part that could explain how this unwelcomed guest had arrived and ended in that position.

I often say to many of my friends that I experience delayed reactions to things that should unearth an impulsive response. That moment was one of them. Fear had long taken wings. There was no desire to even run or scream. I felt like I was ready to fight. This was a David and Goliath moment and I needed that one stone.

I got up and immediately began to think about strategy. My mind experienced another avalanche of questions of a different sort. What do I do first? Is it dead or alive?

My first thought was to open the door and just hit it off. I guess some of you would have been scared to even go near the door, right? Having viewed the territory, I first reached for my phone and became a photographer. I had to capture this snake debacle as maybe no one would believe my story. I opened the door and quickly backed away. The snake did not fall but remained hanging, looking like it had been glued to the door frame.

I wondered. How did it get there? Was it on the top of the door when I had come through the previous evening? Do snakes crawl up? This does not make sense. I took another picture. I went for a broom and touched it. I realized it was dead. With the door wide open, I swung the broom with every strength I had and hit that snake from the door frame. Where it landed I have yet to find out because I searched as hard as I could but did not find it.

By this time, I was in heightened war mode. I sent a message to few friends. Under the picture of the snake hanging from the frame of the open door, I wrote:

Not sure when I crushed this in closing the door. But it reminds me that my enemies will also be destroyed without me doing anything to them. Don't know how or where it could crawl from and get between the door either. I only saw it when it was dead. So shall death come to my enemies in Jesus' name.

One of the accounts I follow on Instagram is "Get through the Week." The affirmation they posted for that day was this:

God is saying to you today, "I know you feel tired, stressed and completely overwhelmed. But know this morning I have your back. I am going to send you a blessing to remind you that I am always in your corner.

That morning I confirmed what I always knew: *God had my back.* I was tired, stressed and overwhelmed because the journey had been quite tumultuous. That last year had fallen nothing short of my World War III. I wrote in my journal:

The snake saga is a powerful experience... God has me.... Just as how I cannot explain the movement of the snake, I can't always predict the moves of the enemy. They are devious...but they can't invade my borders or my space. It will come to nought.

A friend reminded me that Jesus is the door and no one or nothing can come to me unless it comes through Him. You see, there are those experiences that we have that seem to come right out of left field. We are stumped, feel uncertain, and are unprepared for the encounter. But that is when we need to wield our bat and hit that ball with all the strength we have. The Bible says that God's strength is made perfect in my weakness and that morning; I sensed that. Whatever "snake" you wake up to, know that you have something in you to hit it out of your surroundings. Muster every strength that you can, and like I did, sometimes you fight from a place of fear, but do not give up the fight. Clarity will come, the music that causes strength to rise in you may seem faint, but listen, you will hear it.

Yes, you will dance.

2

Lessons from a Tomato Tree

It is said that life is a series of lessons. The settings are not the traditional classroom where there is a lot of chalk and talk, or technology directed learning, but these are experiences that we have in life which we often overlook, and in so doing, can miss valuable lessons or reminders. This sometimes happens because our lives can become such a roller coaster of activities that we do not stop to get in touch with our experiences and the people around us.

In carrying out my daily tasks, stressed, feeling overworked, and ending the day feeling sapped and drained were becoming all too familiar. My days were beyond full and at one point, those external to my workplace told me that I was "wearing too many hats." The responsibilities were not chosen but rather came with the territory. I made it work the best way I could and somehow managed to develop coping strategies. I kept many things private and was selective with how and where I chose to be cathartic as the right support and advice were needed. There was one thing I was sure of; this could not continue. I held dear the circumstances and confirmations when I had made the transition and I was confident I would make the exit at the right time.

Reading, watching television, playing online games, journaling, and spa trips are among the many things that some of us do to unwind. One of my de-stressors and therapeutic activities became the planting of a kitchen garden. It felt good going into the garden after work, tending the plants, watching them grow, blossom and bear fruit. When I started this garden, I did something that I could not recall ever doing. I prayed over it and asked God to allow it to be a witness of His blessing and provision in my life.

One day, I noticed a small tomato plant growing in one of the containers where I had recently turned over and dug up the soil to plant some fresh seeds. I had not planted any tomato seeds since those of the previous year had not thrived. This tender plant was evidence that I had stirred up seeds that did not germinate. I watched the plant grow into a healthy tree. In fact, it was the healthiest tree in the kitchen garden and had put out many blossoms.

One very windy weekend, the salty air, blown over from the sea nearby, burned off many of its leaves and blossoms. I was disappointed as I was looking forward to a great harvest. Despite that, the tree never died. It continued to grow while I watered it. I was delighted when I saw it had put out two lovely tomatoes. I cared for them like a young baby and was excited as I watched them grow and mature. It was a satisfying moment when I picked them both. They were the healthiest and most natural looking tomatoes I had seen in a while, and being organic, it was a sumptuous and tasty addition to my salad.

As I reflected on the experiences related to that tomato tree, a number of lessons came to my mind. The fact that the seed germinated after almost a year of being planted reminded me of the timing of events in our lives. In 2019, I bought a book, *God Meant It for Good*, authored by R. T. Kendall. I had this book lying around and had not read it. In the summer of 2021, I started reading the book. It illustrated the story of Joseph in the Bible with some focus on the verse in particular, Genesis 50:20. This was in reference to the actions of his brothers that what they meant for evil, God meant it for good. There were so many powerful lessons I learned as I read that book. I was experiencing my own time of questioning evil seasons in my life, and I realized it was the perfect timing for reading that book, despite having bought it two years ago.

Sometimes delays and setbacks can cause us to become frustrated and distressed. When we set goals, there can be setbacks, but timing matters. This tree reminded me that I should not allow any vice or force to destroy what was meant to bear fruit in my life. *Who you are, and what is in you, cannot be taken away unless you choose to surrender and give up during a stormy season in your life.* The salty sea air that destroyed some of the blossoms and leaves did not destroy the entire plant. There were blossoms that remained as evidence that fruit-bearing was still a possibility. The tree had continued to grow until it bore fruits.

Nurture what is in you. Read, meditate, share with others, and do not forget your talents and potential. Remember that in the toughest times, something can happen that brings fruit in your life. Don't forget that when there is growth and acceleration in different areas of your life, things like the salty air will come as attacks and setbacks, but it cannot totally destroy what is in you. Find the strength to nurture what is growing. Fruit will come! Things do not always work out in the time we expect, but like nature, life has its seasons.

The popular thinking that *nothing happens before the time* is echoed and used by many of us at different points. Sometimes, after disappointing encounters, we use it as a comfort. At other times, it is to celebrate something that has finally happened. Victory is sweet. I love comeback stories. I love to see the underdog triumph. Situations can arise that seem to threaten where you're headed. You invest time and effort, and you don't see the returns.

Where there is life, there is hope, is another well-used concept that can help us to ride over those seasons. The beauty seen in the growth of the plant from a seed that had been buried reminded me that those skills, talents and potential deposited in our lives can always grow and become a testimony and a blessing. Things may seem delayed. Everyone in your circle seems to be moving ahead and you feel left behind. Do not be discouraged, because what is in us cannot be destroyed if we nurture it. Your season will come.

Sowing seeds is a faith experience and something to be practiced. These seeds can take different forms—a helping hand, a listening ear, financial support, educational pursuits are just a few. Sometimes we do not always see immediately the fruits of what we have done. However, continue to do good and maintain a positive spirit. Fight on and aim to overcome the moments of frustration. I have come across the popular statement repeatedly with the idea that *you thought you had buried me, but you did not know that I was a seed.* Once there is a seed there's always the possibility of growth. Don't let the snake of discouragement cause you to give up. Keep dancing! Turn over the soil in places where you have sown seeds as you prepare for a new season of sowing. There is no telling what you will unearth. Buried seeds within you can still grow.

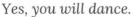

Yes, *you will dance.*

Epilepsy Pain

There is no one I have encountered who enjoys being ill or experiencing pain, except for someone who may be suffering from a factitious disorder (a mental disorder in which someone deceives others by appearing sick) or has masochistic tendencies. Self-care, annual checkups, doctors' visits are practices maintained by many in the quest to stay healthy. Although these are preventative and recommended practices, this does not exclude us from facing health issues. I had my personal encounter.

The all too familiar feeling engulfed me. I looked around trying to recall where I was. My head felt heavy as I sat dazed and slowly struggled to adjust my thoughts as I waited for complete consciousness. My mother sat looking at me and then asked the all too familiar question, "how are you feeling?" I groaned the usual response, "I am ok," as I didn't know what else to say. I was coming out of yet another seizure. I feared it would never end and I would have to live with this health challenge.

The ongoing battle with epilepsy began during my fourth form year of high school (Grade 10). It came unexpectedly. There was no known family history. The episodes were characterized by loss of consciousness, falling and at times I even wet myself. There was a haunting discomfort and general weakness for the following two to three days after which I would begin to feel like my normal self. I had been to numerous doctors, and despite tests, various medications, and interventions, nothing seemed to help. I visited general practitioners, psychiatrists, psychologists, and various medical specialists. I was diagnosed with *petit mal seizures*. The speculations as to the cause were rife.

I secretly harbored feelings of pain and disappoint-ment every time I had an episode and wondered why this had to be happening. I never voiced my feelings, but sometimes I secretly prayed that it would all end either way. In fact, I was embarrassed to even talk about this illness. I didn't want anyone to know what was happening to me as it seemed that I was always being pitied. Many of the comments, though well-intentioned, broke my spirit.

Those petit mal seizures had no early enough warning signs and I knew they were ready to throw me into pain just moments before the blow. The approaching feelings of losing consciousness were scary. The corner of my eyes twitched, and I wished I could wipe away the grayness that was enveloping me. If I was around family who understood, they knew that the blank stares were an indication that there was going to be a seizure and they would protect me from any hurt, the best way they could. I never shared if I was sensing an attack, I just tried to make myself safe and free from any objects that would hurt me. This really could not be for a lifetime. In hindsight, I wondered why I had accepted it as so.

I recall one incident that occurred when the doctors changed my medication. Following the first dose, I had an adverse reaction. I can still hear and see my mother's frustration as she took the bottle of tablets, stood at the back door, and hurled them over into the bushes. In pain she exclaimed, "God, yuh gimme har, it betta yuh tek har back than me see har a suffa suh". (God, you gave her to me, so it's better for you to take her back than for me to see her suffer in this way). That was the last doctor's visit I had.

I was on and off medication until my college years. During the beginning semester of my first year, I had two episodes that almost ended my college sojourn. I woke one night to find my room full of dorm mates. My roommate later explained what had happened and once more the feeling of dejection swallowed me. The following morning, I woke and recalled heading to the bathroom, but when I regained consciousness, I was at the doctor. Consequently, my parents were called, and I was sent home. I returned after a week. In one of my classes, I recalled some hesitation on the part of the lecturer about my participation in a presentation. I detected she was concerned that I may not have been strong enough. Although I felt fine, one of my close friends later shared how gaunt and pale I had looked when I resumed classes.

Another college mate shared how she was looking through her dorm room window one day and felt like coming down to the wash area where she saw me. She later recounted that she was just in time to prevent me from falling headlong into the sink, again from a seizure attack. Despite this, God's hand was still on my life, and my calling as an educator was not thwarted. I was able to graduate as class valedictorian.

On another occasion, I was at home. Then, I was living alone. I sensed that an episode was coming on and I attempted to get to the bed to lie down but did not make it. I damaged my left eye as I got a wound from falling on the clothes iron that was on the floor. I had to seek medical attention and ended up wearing a bandage over my eye. On my way from the doctor, one man whom I did not know looked at me and stated: "What a way fe yuh man r**s yuh in a fe yuh yeye." (It seems your boyfriend has punched you in your eye). Doubtless to say I felt humiliated as this was said in earshot of everyone in the town square. I hurt deep down, and I had to restrain myself from allowing tears to run down my face.

There were many painful experiences that followed me throughout the years, but I continued my life and daily activities, with all the dreams and pursuits that I envisioned. In completing my first degree, I relocated to Kingston. Many thought I should not live alone, and they expressed concerns every time I had an episode. As a result, I sometimes kept them hidden.

One weekend while living in Kingston, I had yet another seizure. Even though I was experiencing the usual episode hangover, I still went to church. My pastor at the time, noticed that I did not seem to be my usual self and questioned what had happened. I shared with him what was happening to me and explained that it happened every time I had my seizure.

Like Jesus speaking to the disciples in the boat, asking them why they were fearful, he asked me, "Why are you owning these seizures? Did God give them to you? They are not yours! Stop owning them! Change the way you speak!"

I was startled as no one had ever spoken to me like that before. He summoned some other officers of the church; they formed a circle around me, anointed me with oil and prayed in the name of Jesus. From that day in 1998, I have never had another seizure. I can praise God!

I learned that I can dance my way through what I say, reaffirming life and death are in the power of the tongue (Proverbs 18:21). I can speak peace. I can renounce negativity. We can declare victory over the situations we face. Just as the petit mal seizures appeared, it is the same way in which they can disappear. It was a painful season, but it was not without vital lessons learned. I can empathize and identify with those who have walked this route. Even though it was difficult, and I still don't understand why, I can look back and see God's hand preserving me.

There is one dominant reality that has never escaped my thoughts—Illness, unexpected medical emergencies and failing health are a part of our day-to-day experiences. We battle strange diseases, face surgeries, take medication and there are illnesses that we just cannot explain how we became affected. Many of us have watched friends and loved ones struggle through various health challenges and treatment episodes. We can recall hospitalization and various interventions. Many of us as Christians have travailed in prayer, trusting God for the miraculous, yet the illness continues. Sometimes healing comes through death, and the unanswered questions remain in our minds, and we ask God why. Sickness is one of those painful moments of life, and I have had my experience. Thankfully, over 20 painful years of battling seizures now lay behind me.

Yes, I *danced!*

6

The Moves

Life was never designed to be a static experience as we encounter various movements at different scenes on life's stage. We move from one home, church, community, country, or job to another. We change diets, gym registration, cars, doctors, and friends as we seek to facilitate the dreams and desires we have. With moves come experiences, and with experiences come emotional, mental, and spiritual encounters that we have to process.

I recall so many hurdles as I moved through the different scenes of my own experiences. I faced many crossroads of serious decision-making. I battled with how unfair life gets sometimes. This was not only in my professional life but in my social exchanges and my Christian walk. I grew up in a Christian home and my father was an avid churchgoer and dedicated lay preacher. I saw his battles and learnt valuable lessons from him about standing up for what was right. I saw commitment lived out in his service although I did not agree with all the decisions and sacrifices he made. He was selfless and was for me the epitome of the adage, *whatever is worth doing, is worth doing well*. His love for people was his motivation and he displayed the strength to look above all else to serve well. A year after leaving teachers' college, and beginning my professional journey, his precious life of 70 years and three months closed on July 21, 1991.

The workplace can sometimes be a serious battleground. The conflicts can involve issues such as the denial of a promotion, coworker tensions, management, or administrative issues, all of which have the potential to be explosive depending on how we choose to process or work through the related dynamics. I accepted though, that no conflict, no abuse of power could rob you of any gifts that God deposited in you. Many times, we fight against what seems unfair and it sometimes can cause such emotional distress that we may even become sick. I have learnt the value of choosing my battles. I also know that sometimes you may not be able to dance through a situation as you want to, but no battle lasts forever. Fight on and listen out for the music that will make you take the floor and perform the newest dance move of overcoming.

My journey includes moves that have been diverse and tumultuous at points. I graduated from teachers' college as class valedictorian and was offered a job at the same school where I did my teaching practice. Needless to say, after four years, I was still in a temporary position with no clear reason why this was so, and no indication of when this would change. The details causing this fell nothing short of the abuse of power. The decision to fight against what was a deliberate and calculated leadership decision had all the marks of being nasty and so I moved on.

My next post was at my alma mater. I worked for three years and then moved on by choice, as I relocated in my pursuit of further studies. Following its successful completion, I initially found employment in a temporary post. It eventually led to a permanent appointment where I served that institution for a few months shy of six and a half years, leaving as the Head of my Department. I then headed toward my first experience working overseas.

This was again another divinely orchestrated move, as when I initially interviewed for the post, I was two courses short of completing post graduate studies. I was unable to assume the position at the required time, so I saw it as a missed opportunity. Interestingly, on completion of those courses, I learned that there were two unexpected resignations at the institution that needed to be filled right away. I qualified for both. They again placed the offer on the table, which I accepted. I began an interesting new season on January 1, 2005, when I relocated to another country. This was a brief stint because I resigned after six months and returned home that summer.

Prior to my leaving, I had applied for placement in the public school system, and within a year, I had returned to assume duties as a teacher of Mathematics. This had an interesting start as I was interviewed and deployed as a teacher of English. When I met with the principal on the first day, she was elated to discover that I was trained and qualified in both areas. The need for the Math teacher was greater, so an immediate switch was made.

The next eleven years of my professional journey were bittersweet. I gained the thrills of personal development and myriad of opportunities to do presentations involving various areas on the educational spectrum. I rose to Head of Department, but the journey was not without a bevy of challenges. I experienced the overt and subtle marginalization associated with being a 'foreigner'; the misconceptions brewed from cliques at work and the claws of control and manipulation of authority.

Despite all of those, I did not lose my dance steps, as I made great friends and relationships, some of which are still a part of my life. I left those precincts for another opportunity in a different overseas locale, the place of my snake dream and encounter.

Those moves were strategic and well timed. Not once did I feel like I was off course. I reaped a harvest of experiences that have served as lifelong lessons not only for me, but many with whom I have shared them. Despite the many battles, the mental struggles, and the anguish, I always clung to one reality—*there is better ahead.* I never stopped yearning and looking for open doors. Each opportunity exceeded the previous in a myriad of ways. Time and again I watched God make things beautiful in his time (Ecclesiastes 3:11) in my life. I learned to trust God's hand and look away from people's expectations and their timelines for my life.

I have lost some battles. I made choices at times out of fear, being misinformed, angry, frustrated, or getting even. There were moments I just wanted to lock myself away. I vented. I cussed. I cried. Yet, I never settled for what I knew I did not want. I chose to find my music and dance.

Yes, I *danced!*

7

Battered, Bruised yet Bouncing Back

Popular poet and author Maya Angelou says, "You may not control all the events that happened to you, but you can decide not to be reduced by them." I lived this reality as I looked back over my life, reliving the last few years in a new country and a new working environment. Some seasons seemed like I was watching a movie. Shortly after assuming a new position at work, I was forced to have knee surgery. The sudden and repeated swellings on my knee revealed that tumors were growing on the lining. Thankfully, they were benign, and healing/

recovery was swift. Not having the smooth start that I had wanted, I felt like I had been thrown into a warzone. My journal became that friend who would celebrate with me, cry with me, and laugh with me when I sat alone at the end of each day to reflect. Its pages told many stories.

> My life has been a whirlwind of activities. I am adjusting ... all its demands, knee surgery and so much more. I feel far from settled and on top of things. All this paperwork and correspondence...I must pray....

In his book *Tough Times Never Last, but Tough People Do*, Robert Schuller shares a number of principles that can be used to help us bounce back from difficult situations. That needed power he feels lies within us. The proverbial end of the rope feeling, is one that most of us can identify with in our own experiences. Those moments when it seems that you can't go on, can sometimes be eclipsed by the reminder of a former hardship that you encountered and overcame. This reminder serves as a crutch for your fallen spirit causing you to push on looking for a brighter day. There is this verse in the Bible that addresses the reality of hard times and celebrates the spirit of the overcomer. In II Corinthians 4:8-9, the apostle Paul captures it well, "We've been surrounded and battered by troubles, but we're not demoralized..." (Message Bible).

I read a lot when I am going through tough times. I tend to focus on books that relate to the present situation. *This Present Darkness* is an old novel by Frank Perretti and I was reading it at a point that must have been the darkest season of my professional career. I read the book like my survival depended on it. I read with heightened shock, mixed with delight, at the unfolding of scheme after scheme. I saw the attempts to distort information and manipulate people in an attempt to shut down a Christian school, but I also saw the power of prevailing prayer. I saw weakness turned to strength. I saw well planned plots exposed and fall apart one after the other and it sounded all so familiar.

During an unsettling season in my experience at one of the institutions where I served, a group of people whom I knew and some of whom I worked with, orchestrated a series of events that was aimed at what I would describe as character assassination. I suspected the expectation was probably that when it all unfolded, I would resign or yield to the pressure to comply with the demands that were being dished out to me. They were relentless. The schemes rained like hard blows from my opponent in a boxing match, but when it seemed I was knocked out, I was back on my feet before the count was out.

One day, I was made aware of letters that were written and shared in different arenas. These letters defamed me and made accusations that had no supporting evidence. Though these were un-substantiated and at best spurious, I felt pained at the depths to which people went to show hatred and resentment.

One letter was signed by a number of people and another one was distributed to institutions that had direct bearing on my work and status as an expatriate. I was gutted, but God provided the right group of supporters including my employers who could vouch for the truth of my service. Their written response was more than a buffer, and it countered the meanness that had been penned by my detractors. I felt proud as I read of the confidence they had in me, and the detailed description of how I had carried out my duties. They meant it for evil, but God used it for my good. I know in that season, unseen hands carried me, and I never ran. I summed it up by saying every attempt was being made to pull the mat from under my feet, but I never fell.

In my journal I wrote:

Yesterday's visit ... was nonsense at the highest level. I honestly thought it was over, but I realize they have not let up. Lies and schemes ... But I stand as a tree by the rivers of water (Psalm 1):

- I will bring forth fruit.
- What I do will prosper.
- My leaves will not wither.
- The chaff will be driven away.

Lord I will continue until you say stop.

Bitterness is a chosen response to unfair attacks. Joseph faced and survived the jealousy of his brothers, and the false accusation of his employer's wife, which resulted in him being imprisoned, and his ministry to fellow prisoners was forgotten. All of this did not destroy the purpose for which Joseph was created and why he ended up in Egypt. The dream of his juvenile years was fulfilled as he rose to lead Egypt through one of the most crucial seasons of its existence. His brothers indeed had to bow down to him. Although he did not understand his dreams initially, the unfolding was testimony to what God had destined for him. I learned that despite the bevy of attacks, what lay in me could not be destroyed.

What many did not know was that my decision to serve in that institution was not a frivolous one. God used someone to confirm this move in a prayer session. It came at a time when I wanted to leave where I was working. I was unsure of what to do when a friend of mine shared the staff opening. I sent an application and as they say, the rest is history. I came to the institution at a time when my skill set, and knowledge base were exactly what was needed. The timing was right on all levels. Therefore, I knew that I could not just run. I had to serve and make the exit when I sensed my service was complete.

I survived verbal threats, the unleashing of expletives from angry people, those who used defense mechanisms in a bid to transfer blame, and those who hated me because they claimed, "their spirit did not take to me." I experienced what it feels like to walk into church and be stripped by stares, to see people peering into my face wondering if I was really smiling, to see students being used as weapons, and being called evil by those responsible for my spiritual welfare. I battled with the Lord about so many things. I couldn't see what was ahead, but I knew God was leading me. I wondered when it would end. Sometimes, despite the celebrations of the school and the strides we were making, I found myself living in anticipation of the next onslaught.

On the journey, I always had timely reminders that helped me to refocus. I recall having a team visit the school to do special services for a few days. One of the speakers shared a series of lessons based on the book of Esther in the Bible. Although I have read and listened to messages on the story on many occasions, I was never captured by the phrase "Mordecai sat" (Esther 6:12) until that morning when he spoke. This posture is mentioned ten times in that Old Testament book, and as emphasized by the speaker, was one of resolution. There were no tantrums, no fuss, save waiting at the place where he knew help would come. That morning was a reminder that I needed to just sit in God's presence and wait for Him to move.

I saw God remove and replace people. I saw those who were plotting together turn against each other. On one occasion, I had a meeting which I knew could become nasty because of what was going to be addressed. This somehow fell through, and I had to deliver a letter with content that had the potential to be explosive. I delayed for no clear reason except that my spirit sensed that I should hold off on delivering it.

On the day when I intended to hand it over, the person resigned, removing every opportunity for a fire. God proved He was with me yet again. The Psalms are replete with instances of David pouring out His heart and crying to the Lord in difficult situations, and I read many of these repeatedly. The popular lines from the lyrics of Babbie Mason's song, "When you can't trace his hand, trust his heart," became more meaningful.

When I eventually made the decision to resign, it shocked many people. The wars had ceased, and all seemed settled. I gave no explanations except the one statement that it was necessary that I return to my homeland. Nothing or no one could make me change my mind. I even surprised myself by the resolute stance, but I knew it was right and the timing was perfect. The only tug at my heart was that I was in the middle of a contract, and I would be breaking it. I refused to battle through the what-ifs, one more year, or the wrong timing drama. I was not going to relent.

The resolution was timely, and I completed my contract. I could make my exit with a feeling of satisfaction and expectation regarding what open doors lie ahead. The Bible story of Joseph reminded me that I must give God the freedom to do it in His way and in His time. I must take my hands off. The battle is His. This takes faith.

Another entry from my journal shares my thoughts:

I am a diamond in the rough. He is still chiseling away at my life as He fashions and shapes me to reflect His beauty. There is so much wrapped up inside of me. I am sometimes misunderstood, judged, attacked, and ridiculed. I don't always get it right, but I know he is still working on me ....

Tornadoes! Tropical storms! Hurricanes! Cyclones! Snowstorms! These are weather systems that have battered many countries, leaving loss of lives and significant damages, yet nations and people have bounced back. Divorce, heartbreak, cancer diagnosis, loss of a job, and the foreclosure on the home are just some examples of things and experiences that have battered us emotionally. Yet we forge on, even when recovery and bouncing back are real struggles.

These situations can sometimes leave you feeling like the man on the Jericho Road who was robbed, beaten, and left for dead as told in the story recorded in the Bible in Luke 10. Lying battered and bruised, there came the Good Samaritan, who cleaned his wounds and carried him to a place of treatment. There are still Good Samaritans; you don't have to live in brokenness. I survived the battering. I healed from the bruises. I felt like I wanted to throw in the towel, but there were Good Samaritans at various points on the journey. Sometimes it was a lonely feeling, but I never lost hope.

Yes, I *danced!*

8

I'm Single: Don't Make it a Pain

My mother has always held some concerns about me remaining single. This has been voiced to different people in varying ways and at different times. On my first decision to work overseas in 2005, she gave me some advice in that regard. She affirmed that she knew I was sensible and told me that if I found someone who wanted to marry me, I should give it some consideration. I should give him the test and if he passed it, then I should know what to do. I am not sure what that test was, but that was her way of warning me against any irrational and careless mate choosing.

Like most females, I had my dreams of courtship, marriage, and a happy family with children. I even secretly dreamed of having twins as I have twin uncles, twin nephews, and twin cousins. I was deeply conscious that marriage and building a family were not something to be forced, and despite what was happening around me with friends and family in this regard, I never felt that it was a movement that I should ensure I got caught up in. I never saw it as mandatory either. If you are a church girl like me, then you may be able to identify with the pressure that sometimes comes from that institution, especially among those who feel like this is a milestone that needs to be achieved.

I have loved and I have dated. I have had my share of disappointments but have in no way felt like I have lost. At one point, it seemed that marriage was on the books, because from all indications, the guy I was dating, seemed like he would be my future husband. It didn't happen and I don't consider myself any less than those who are happily married. I have, however, gained invaluable wisdom and experience as it relates to male-female relationships. Friends come and go. We date or we don't. We fall in and out of love. It's all in the game of life.

Never in my wildest dreams, however, did I ever imagine that remaining single and not being a biological mother could carry such a stigma. The confrontations have varied from cynicism to outright rudeness and disrespect. I recall on one occasion, being scoffed at, and asked, "Missies, yuh nah guh breed?" (Hey, aren't you going to have a child?). One of my sisters told me that my response should be that babies are not like clothes that have to be worn. I have had people grab my hands and ask me where the ring is. I have encountered those who expressed pity as if I was not living. On many occasions, I had to muster self-control and avoid hurling insults or angry statements at the insensitivity I faced.

During my postgraduate studies in Counseling Psychology, we had various course requirements which involved group work and presentations. One involved an assignment in the Marriage and Family Therapy module. A group of about five or six of us did a presentation we entitled "Single, Sassy and Satisfied." We enacted a group of single women at a retreat sharing together on how to live fulfilled lives. Among the things that were done was watching Juanita Bynum's message 'No More Sheets.' This was well received as the variety of discussions seemed to land home with the majority of the class. We explored all sides of the coin as it relates to singleness and contentment.

At this juncture in my life, that presentation title still holds true. Singleness is not equal to misery, loss or unfulfilled living. I am satisfied with where I am in life. I have loved and been hurt, but never willed myself to feel miserable or unaccomplished. Sitting around and moping was never my resolve. Instead, I have made my life count. I work hard and I play hard. I have learned to make time for myself. I travel and take annual vacations. I love my spa treatments, whether it's a visit to a facility or a self-created one at home. I have my times of treating myself to something special and sometimes I do splurge. I reward myself, and self-care has taken on new meaning in my life.

The reality is, I believe marriage was never meant for everyone. While I embrace the belief that it is a great institution, nothing is wrong if you are not in a marriage bond. Self-love is applicable for both married and single people. The apostle Paul says I have learned in whatever state I am to be content (Philippians 4:11). Singleness is not a crime! My singleness is nothing that I am ashamed of, and so I dance in contentment.

I do not want you to think that I am anti-marriage. Far from it. I have seen friends marry early and have great families. I have seen the reverse where the marriage just never worked out. I have also seen the pain of childlessness in committed relationships. Growing up in a Christian family and making a decision to serve the Lord early in my life governed my actions. I'll admit I have made poor choices and decisions along the way, but who doesn't at some point in their lives.

The Bible has varying accounts of single women, some having never been married and some became widows. There are also accounts of childlessness among couples. When one's marital status is not viewed from a correct perspective, there can be hurt emotions and destroyed relationships. This view can be from the single individual or by those responding to it. Sarah was childless and it bothered her. Despite God's promise of a child and that her husband Abraham would be a father of many nations, Sarah came up with her own solution. She encouraged Abraham to sleep with the maid Hagar, but when she became pregnant, Sarah felt she was being ridiculed, and drove Hagar out of the home.

Hannah in the book of Samuel, was teased repeatedly by Peninnah because she was childless. She spent many hours in prayer until God blessed her with a child. Mary was single at the time of conception with Jesus, and what a community embarrassment that could have been. You see, whether single or married, we need to be sure that our decisions are not driven by what others say or think of us. Be guided by moral and godly principles.

There are childless couples who have adopted or fostered children. Single people have shared their experiences and empower others who are struggling. My life is my story, the path I know has been God-ordained. I have not missed out. My life is not unfulfilled because I have not done what is considered a part of life, married with children. I celebrate who I am, having survived being berated, and being stalked and insulted when I allowed my values to guide my relations. I am single, sassy and satisfied.

Yes, I *dance!*

9

Out of Left Field

I doubt that any of us will live to a point where we can truly say, *nothing surprises me anymore.* My mind travels back to the shock the world experienced with news of the sudden and tragic death of renowned basketball player, Kobe Bryant, and his daughter. That really came out of left field and even though there were millions who had never met Bryant in person, his prowess on the basketball court had earned him fans globally.

Life has those moments and many of us have been there. We experience the suddenness of events such as unexpected deaths, false accusations, sudden illnesses, job loss or some crisis that really disrupt the normal flow of things or proverbially 'rock the boat'. We use expressions such as, "I can't believe" or "I must be dreaming" to give voice to our feelings. Emotions in those situations can push us over the edge if we are not careful, and an ill-timed or knee jerk reaction may not necessarily work for our good. Hence, in those 'out of left field' moments the need to exercise self-control or restraint is vital.

Although there are many views as to what does or does not create these surprises, life will have these moments. Some surprises are pleasant, others painful, some unearth anger while some seem to throw life into a tailspin. At some point, we have had one of these surprises. Our responses indicate how we process it.

One morning, I was checking email, as I prepared for the day. The contents of each were among the norm except for this special one. I read the email over and over. I checked the sender. This could not be. I contended silently. I read the entire thread. I sat down. The scathing contents made me feel almost nauseated. I sat down and pondered my response. I was reading an email about me that was not meant for me. The contents were all but complimentary and I did not know why I was being accused in that way. I battled with the anger that was rising and realized I had to control my thoughts and emotions if I were going to handle it without saying or doing anything that I would regret. The moment was unsettling.

This was indeed a case of what was done in the dark coming into light. I began to analyze the encounter and realized the attack. When a snake attacks, it first chews its prey then brings it to the back of its mouth where the venom is released from the fang's bite. I was feeling the bitterness from both the sender and the receiver involved in the exchange. The person who had sent the email was engaging in another smear campaign. I knew I needed to dance no matter what and I was going to find the right music.

I confronted and it did not go well. The response was cold and uncaring, and I was asked to dismiss the mail as it was not meant for me, but the error in sending it to my inbox was an eye-opener for me. This was not the only email that would have been sent but every attempt was exposed, and the desired end was never achieved. This was not without some intense battles.

These were just a smattering of many surprising encounters. On another occasion, I was asked to alter a document. I refused! The tirade that followed was so fierce that I wondered if it was perceived that I had lost my sense of ethical conduct. Each stance I took seemed to prompt another scheme and I wondered when it would end. By now, a movement seemed to have been growing as there were those who were determined to destroy me professionally, mentally and emotionally. The onslaughts were rapid and unpredictable, but God remained faithful and God's charge to Joshua was like medicine to an ailing heart. "Be strong and courageous." I am ever grateful for my praying friends. I know what it means to be carried on the wings of prayer.

There is a litany of things that I could detail, some of which would make you cry or just giggle, like that day when a student put a lizard in her math notebook and handed it in for grading. I was naive to the fact that some students were lingering around not for grades but to see my reaction. Can you imagine me opening the book and seeing a lizard alive and laying as if cornered? I flung the book, screamed, and ran outside. My then supervisor still laughs uncontrollably as she recounts seeing me running down the corridor to her office.

One of the greatest struggles during one of these bitter periods was that some of my assailants included people in whom I had invested time and resources, at varying levels. I felt betrayed. But I learnt through pain to accept the reality that sowing seeds does not always bring the harvest that you envision. There are all types of soils and every person responds differently. While some may be appreciative, reciprocation is never guaranteed. Not reaping in one ground does not always mean you wasted your seed, as we sometimes experience bumper harvests in others. Sowing seeds does not mean it will always be nurtured. Many times, we don't see hearts, we see needs, and we sow.

My trust in people waned and I struggled against becoming bitter. But just like how we see the sun peeping out after the rain, there was always something or someone that came as a reminder that it would not last forever. The "I never saw this coming" moments of our lives can really knock the 'winds out of our sails.' Using the game of cricket as an analogy, we choose whether to make a stroke or leave the 'ball' alone. Those balls can come in the forms of bouncers, Yorkers, leg spinners, or off spinners. The key is how we face the balls.

The value of support, a listening ear, or some means of managing your response is needed. Sometimes we may want a time of solitude to regain our composure or settle our emotions. In the Bible, there is the account of Job who encountered a tsunami of 'balls' out of left field. He lost family, health, and possessions.

Friends accused him and passed judgment, but Job echoed words that many of us have quoted in our difficult times. "He knows the way that I take: when he has tested me, I shall come forth as gold" (Job 23:10, NKJV).

In God there is no left field. Nothing catches Him off guard so we can always cast our cares and concerns on Him. His eyes run to and fro throughout the earth on the behalf of those that fear Him, and He delivers them (2 Chronicles 6:9). You will feel swamped! If you react inappropriately, or become depressed and overwhelmed, seek to lift yourself and regain strength and composure.

Share with a trusted friend, and above all hold on to the promises of God's Word. God is not surprised or shocked because He knows the plans He has for you. These plans are to give you hope and a future (Jeremiah 29:11). Rest in that assurance and allow that to strengthen you when those 'balls' come at you from left field.

I faced many balls, bowled at varying speeds on different pitches. I never always knew how to face them, but I never ran away from the games. I survived many experiences from left field.

Yes, I danced!

Surviving Snake Land: Fight or Flight?

L iving with snakes is not the norm. There are special places and geographical locations that are natural habitats for snakes. One such place is the Narcisse Snake Dens that can be found in the region of Manitoba in Canada. According to National Geographic, this is said to be the place where there is the largest gathering of snakes worldwide. The climate and geology of the area lend themselves to being the perfect habitat for red-sided garter snakes. This is a tourist attraction. Those who visit are able to survive the experience because they follow the instructions of the tour guide. They go where they're told, touch where they can, and for those who feel scared, they stay at a safe distance.

In Africa, there are various traditions among different tribes, one of which includes snake dancing. There is a notable tribe in Tanzania which is called the Zigua Tribe. Viewing their interactions with snakes for me is spine-chilling, as it includes snakes such as the black mamba, pythons, and boomslangs which are all venomous. Some have been defanged so they can be "safely" used in their various activities and dances. The aim of this tribe is to educate people while preserving their land of snakes.

I coined the term snake land as a description of life with the ever-present reality that there will be those places and seasons when we will have encounters that are dangerous and may even seem life threatening. These can come in various forms, and in some cases, can really destroy. Snake lands can be in the home, at work, at school, in the community and even in church and can involve those whom we never expected. Families can be torn apart, marriages broken, churches split, and lifetime friendships broken. In those experiences we have to choose if we are going to fight or take our flight, knowing that the general goal is to survive.

One day I caught up with a friend whom I had lost touch with for a few years. We re-established contact and tried to catch up and share the developments in our lives. She was unaware, however, of the details of my current situation. One morning, she called and with some amount of concern and a bit fearful, said she had a dream about me. Disturbing as it sounded, there was an element of dancing in it that made me smile. What was interesting, was that the setting of her dream was the same as mine.

This time, however, it was not snakes but frogs. Which is worse? I can't decide as I find both equally repulsive. She related that these frogs had raised heads, and I immediately remembered the snakes in my dream, but she detailed that their opened mouths turned out to resemble those of alligators. What a sight! I thought. She noted, however, that despite the opened mouths, she saw me just stepping on the back of each fearlessly. Having stepped on everyone, I walked back into my house with an air of confidence.

"Whoa! What a dream!" I responded. This undoubtedly took me right back to my personal dream, and I wondered if it was a reminder that the battles would continue, but victory was sure. My own analysis/interpretation was that the alligator-mouthed frogs were symbolic of deception. Considering what was happening at the time, it's the back stepping moves that did it for me. Once again, I was buoyant and felt that the enemies' plans were yet again ousted by the sword of God's promised protection.

I learned that when we receive these messages, they are not just an opportunity for us to tout evil and wickedness, or that we are right in saying people are unkind, schemish, and mean. God is reminding us that we are living and walking in victory despite the fact that there is always evil in the world. The attacks, though overwhelming, do not render us losers or defeated, unless we walk away from the hedge that God provides for us. Job never lost faith, and in the end, he was able to experience restoration in far greater measure than what he had lost.

My snake land experiences are varied. I was surprised when I made some discoveries. Being lied about, slandered and verbally attacked can really sting. For me, it cuts deep. I recall how some encounters left me feeling angry, disappointed and surprised. I struggled with resentment at some points. The fight or flight struggle consumed me many times. I cried unshed tears. I questioned purpose and seasons in my life.

One night, I was so overcome that I felt that was it. I was done. Two of my friends were on the phone with me as I made the reservation for a vacation. They empathized and prayed with me, but never once told me to change my mind. They remained just shoulders to cry on and ears to listen. That trip turned out to be a nice getaway, and I returned to continue the battle for survival.

On one occasion, I tried to wrap my head around the way I had been snubbed and disrespected by someone I mentored and guided. I had no idea what had caused it. I am not sure why I let it hurt the way it did. I felt let down. I decided though, that I was surely not going to wallow because my steps were turned into dancing feet. I stood in front of the bathroom mirror and did a little self-talk.

Before the evening was out, the truth was made clear, and I faced the reality of deception that was unexplainable. My attempts at nurturing, building, giving advice and all else, were utilized, but I began to sense that my humanness and kindheartedness seemed to have meant little. There would be no reciprocation. The dream came back to me on many occasions, and I began to see the familiar faces emerge in painful ways.

I rehearsed some events as I tried to ease the pain that lingered. I began to build up walls. I carefully selected with whom I shared. My trust in people fluctuated. I learnt the value of the need to forgive so I could gain release. Author and motivational speaker, Les Brown says, "If you are carrying strong feelings about something that happened in your past, they may hinder your ability to live in the present." I needed to live and do so with a healthy outlook.

There is a complexity about humans which psychology can never completely explain. Behaviors are unpredictable. The need for cathartic engagements can never be overlooked. We are emotional beings and we all process and respond to our encounters in different ways. Feeling hurt at being disappointed or let down is human. It is never wise to smother or suppress your emotions because you don't want to be seen as weak, unspiritual, or immature. The reality is our responses create opportunities for us to do personal reflection or reach out to someone as we process our emotions. We need to remember that our tribulations differ and that is why for the Bible believer, we are told by Jesus himself, to be of good cheer. Since he overcame, so can we. We all should find our space of healing. It is necessary to remove the venom that we receive in snake land.

There is a life lesson that is pivotal as we experience the ebb and flow of human relationships. This is a test I think I had to take repeatedly as I learnt to navigate the terrain of day-to-day relationships at various levels. Ingratitude, at times, can be painful for one who gives to others. The harsh reality is no one you have helped has any obligation to you. The purity of your intentions will preserve your heart, and you will continue to give and be a blessing. Your reward is sure.

It's interesting that the Bible says we should be wise as serpents and blameless as doves (Matthew 10:16). The lesson is wisdom in our responses, not hurt. Doctors and other health professionals can share countless stories of negative encounters with their clients. Some are rude, have placed blame wrongly, and even brought lawsuits against them, but they are bound by oath not to do harm. Because of that, they can continue to serve other patients. People who are Christians are challenged to walk in love, forgive, and pray for those who harm us. The reality is, you can unknowingly nurture your enemy, but you do not have to be destroyed. I share this journal entry, which was not written during this season of pain. This was one outlet that captured my pain and also provided healing.

When we face our battles ... God does not necessarily reveal all things to us. Sometimes we see a glimmer of the devil's schemes, or we see a glimmer of divine purpose in all that is happening. Yet, at other times, it appears we are blockaded in darkness and fear. But if we allow our minds to recall what God has been doing, we will be able to say unreservedly, 'You did it before, you will do it again,' THE BATTLE IS YOURS!!!

There were many times when I read over my journal entries, and they soothed my spirit. I sometimes laughed, and other times I cried tears of appreciation that God is really an unfailing friend. If we want medicine, we go to the pharmacy. If we want groceries, we visit the supermarket. In our daily interactions we know where to go based on what we need. To survive our snake land experiences, we must face where we have been wounded and seek help. Don't let the venom of the hurt destroy you. I survived and you can too.

Yes, I danced!

Breeding Snakes

The idea of having a snake as a pet is unusual for the majority of us, and it becomes more repulsive when we think of breeding snakes. Engaging with snakes in this way would be absolutely scary for some and downright absurd for others, although there is evidence that both practices are followed by many. For some it's a hobby. There are those who love the concept of having an exotic pet, others are enthusiastic about snakes, while some persons use them in rituals.

Snakes are said to engage in predatory attacks, which is the strategy that is used in preparing to destroy their victims. There is one report of a woman who noticed that her pet snake was losing weight. In discussing this with the veterinarian, she was told that the snake was preparing itself to eventually kill her. This illustrates one of the reasons why breeding or nurturing snakes could result in death. I will go further and ask you: are you a snake breeder?

We can unknowingly breed snakes around us through things and tendencies that have the potential to destroy us. As far-fetched as this may sound for many of us, the reality of nurturing self-destructive practices, or engaging in unhealthy relationships is real. Unchecked, these can cause serious damage. We may be unaware of the growing development, and the revelation can sometimes have devastating effects. When some relationships disintegrate, there can be mental, emotional, and deep psychological scars as a result.

Many times, we are in denial when some negative behaviors or attitudes surface. Out of fear, we are sometimes reluctant to intervene or confront. We ignore the red flags and silently hope things will fix themselves. When we ignore red flags, we are breeding snakes, as the practice that continues without intervention is going to cause hurt or pain to someone.

News reports of family killings, spousal attacks, and student shootings tend to create shock and brokenness on so many levels. In some cases, there were no signs that this could've happened or there were growing signs that were ignored. John F Kennedy, former President of the USA said, "There are risks and costs to a program of action. But they are far less than the long-range risks and costs of comfortable inaction." The need for active evaluation of activities in our lives and those associated with us cannot be overemphasized.

At different junctures, and in different seasons, I had to do some serious self-evaluation. I had to look at some of my habits and relationships and assess the impact they were creating. I realized I was breeding snakes. There were indicators that I needed to desist from some practices and sever ties in others. We need to check ourselves about the practices we have and the behaviors that we model in our different spaces. The need to assess who we talk with and what we talk about is crucial. This applies in the home, at school, in our workplaces, and among those with whom we associate. We have influence wherever we are, and we need to ensure that it is positive, fair, and balanced or we could be breeding snakes.

Psychologist Carl Jung says, "If there is anything that we wish to change in the child, we should first examine it and see whether it is not something that could better be changed in ourselves." If we are seen as schemers by our children, it can become difficult to correct them when they exemplify what they learnt from us.

As leaders, it is important that we do not breed snakes among those under our guidance through partiality or unfair practices. T. D Jakes, world-renowned speaker, and leader, identifies the value of principles and concepts in leadership. In a sermon entitled *Road Rage*, he says, "Uniformed ideas create injustice ... justice must be fair, even, and equitable across the board."

As a leader, I learned to follow policy and practice. It is easier to deal with resentment and dislike that erupt about something you have done when you follow the rules. Leadership requires that you not be a wimp. While you do not exchange sensitivity for rules, there must be guidelines that show consistency in what you do. When someone attacks what you have done, it is easier to address your decisions against the backdrop of established protocols. Uniformity and justice do not breed snakes of our own making, although they can create enemies. The resentment in such a context can be understood.

Boundaries must be maintained, and when we become aware that lines are being crossed and walls of protection are being broken down, we must repair the breach. If this is ignored the potential for breeding snakes arises. Sometimes you may be scoffed at, but self-preservation is important. There are headlines that have been flashed across tabloids, television screens, and various media entities decrying failure of leaders in different ways. Pastors, politicians, husbands, and wives have been caught in compromising situations, or cheating scandals. Homes, churches, and families have sometimes been destroyed in the aftermath of such exposure because snakes were bred through boundary breaches.

Sometimes, just like how people have been destroyed by their pet snake, we breed personal snakes that destroy us. We become self-engaging, jealous, abusive, manipulative, and insensitive. Those habits separate us from others and create tension that is not only self-destructive but can have negative impact on the lives of others. Sometimes we push people away from us and minimize the possibility of building relationships that are necessary for our daily encounters. This reduces the possibility of self-empowerment and the benefits of learning from others. In the book of James, he describes the impact of these habits, not only on us, but others. The Message Bible describes it aptly in my view:

Mean-spirited ambition isn't wisdom. Boasting that you are wise isn't wisdom. Twisting the truth to make yourselves sound wise isn't wisdom. It's the furthest thing from wisdom—it's animal cunning, devilish plotting. Whenever you're trying to look better than others or get the better of others, things fall apart and everyone ends up at the others' throats (James 3:14-16)

Snake breeding is worthy of reflection, and it taught me wisdom. I learnt to retreat. I learnt to self-evaluate. I learnt to repair breaches. I did not want to nurture destructive practices for myself or others. Turkish playwright and novelist Mehmet Murat Idan gives a powerful statement when he says, "The snake produces poison in its body to poison its enemies! But man is a strange snake; he produces poison in his mind to poison his fellow men!"

Because I saw the value of not breeding snakes, I could survive. Where I saw a nest in the making, it was ultimately destroyed. I did not want to produce poison for myself or those with  whom I relate.

Yes,   I   still   danced!

12

Find Your Music and Dance

Plato said, "Music gives a soul to the universe, wings to the mind, flight to the imagination, and life to everything." As I wrote, I became enthralled with some quotations that I read that give voice to the power of music and dancing. If I could identify a common thread, it would be that both music and dance are intertwined. Both give freedom of expression and are sometimes the gateways to the deepest pain or celebrate the greatest moments.

Author and philanthropist Shah Asad Rizvi captures the liberating power of dance when he says: "Burdened no more is the soul for whom life flows through dance like breath." Confucius affirms that "Music produces a kind of pleasure which human nature cannot do without." We waltz, do hip hop, and various dance moves and rituals. Each tells a story. Each carries an emotion. Each is an expression. You cannot dance if there is no music. Music stimulates emotion and prompts a physical response.

There are various music genres that appeal to all of us in different ways. For Caribbean natives, soca, reggae, and dancehall are all too familiar. We listen and dance to them depending on our moods and situations. We use music in our workouts, while we are driving, in our offices, while doing housework, and in so many ways. It is highly unlikely that there would be ska music being played at the interment of a baby unless for a special reason. Music played in the home of a grieving widow differs from that of someone having a party celebrating a promotion. In church, the music during praise and worship differs from that during an altar call.

In writing this book, I read a number of my journals from as far back as the late 1990s. Some of the entries evoked different responses, but there was overarching evidence that journaling was my type of music. I have been able to dance on the pages of these journals echoing my pain, celebrating my achievements, and letting my tears fall because it allowed me to be open and bare my heart. My journals also captured some moves that were out of sync. I realized when I was not dancing, and it caused me to return to the dance floor of God's presence, of prayer and fasting and of seeking godly counsel. Written reflections were not only cathartic but also allowed me to reflect on my walk with the Lord, and to consider what He was saying to me through the Word.

Here is an entry that led me back to His presence.

I cannot trust God to right the wrongs, yet still be fighting a war on the side. If I am confident that my present position and the location is God's purpose, then I must also know that He knows every battle and He has a plan. There is nothing that can happen to me that will take Him off guard, so nothing is outside of His will to change or to rework. I think of:

i. Joseph: He was sold into slavery then imprisoned.

ii. Daniel: He was thrown in the lions' den, yet his life was preserved.

iii. Lazarus was raised from the dead.

I pray: God grant me the grace to trust you more.

I reflect and meditate on Psalms 39 and 40.

Books became music to my soul, my outlet. I gravitated towards anything that described struggle, overcoming victory, and anything that was triumphant. It helped me to realize that life always has moments of pain, but it also has moments of victory. I was always challenged by the means the writer or speaker used to tide them over. Books helped me to dance among the snakes. Books helped me to say to myself, "they did it, I can do it too."

Have you ever woken up any morning with a song in your heart, but got carried away with browsing social media, or some tasks that needed to be done in the house, and just somehow did not have your devotion and meditation? When you were ready you had forgotten that song. Many times, we cannot dance because we have forgotten the music. We have forgotten the song, the tune, and the melody that would put steps in our feet and a lingering song in our hearts. But, when we allow that song to sweep our hearts, we can usher ourselves into a positive mode and can be buoyant and joyful throughout the day. Positive waking thoughts can be the music to which you dance.

I am indebted to one of my older sisters who gave me a bit of advice some time ago. She told me I was taking care of everyone apart from myself and advised me to start traveling more and to take my holidays. That was another outlet. Financially, you may not be able to go to all the places you would want to, but find that thing that gives you a thrill, that will lift your spirit, that is your music. Find it. Dance!

Psychologists, counselors, and coaches espouse balance in our day-to-day activities. Terms like coping skills, me time, and self-care have become more and more commonplace in a fast moving and developing world. The demands of day-to-day work and survival are the places of our battles, and hence we have to find our music. We can easily be engulfed with various demands, and on the flip side, bury ourselves in work or too many commitments in order to mask our pain. That is never the way we were ordained to survive. Taking time for yourself can never be overemphasized. Create your own quiet moment at home. Fill your tub with warm water, add some bath salts, body oils, scented oils and candles with your favorite relaxing music playing and just unwind. I can tell you, it will do you a world of good.

There was a season in my life when I created punchlines that I would utter aloud at various times, usually with a rhythm to which I could dance. There was a line that went viral from a popular game show, where a contestant prayed, "Holy Spirit activate, activate, activate," as she craved divine wisdom in seeking the right answers. You too can create a funny jingle, and dance to it too.

I could not be writing about dancing without including the benefits of dancing. Dance frees the mind and has multiple health benefits. So, I encourage you to plan a dance routine into your day. It may not be every day, maybe three days a week, maybe four days, it may be the first thing you do when you return home from work. You don't need a crowd to dance. Just as some people say they only sing in the bathroom, you can also dance in the "bathroom," that place where you feel free.

Dancing can also alleviate depression. Psychotic episodes can be as a result of negative encounters when they have been prolonged. The emotional and psychological damage can have lifelong consequences if there is no intervention. Dancing is one outlet to release your mind. Create your victory dance and your dancing jingle. Find what works for you. Make that your music.

Think of a mother coming home at the end of the day, tired and drained, sees her little baby, a toddler, grabs that toddler lovingly and begins to dance. I am sure that mother will not remain drained but will be lifted in that moment as there is release, fun, and love. Dance alone. Dance with your partner. Dance into your office in the mornings. Dancing can surprise your coworkers if it's a tough place that you're working in, just dance. Dance even when your heart is broken— dance! Dance! Dance!

Yes, I am still dancing.

13

Leave Footprints When You Dance

The world will remember the historic landing of US airways flight 1549 in the Hudson River on January 15, 2009, after it had come in contact with a flock of geese causing both engines to fail. All lives on board were saved. There are many other events that can be identified as heroic due to the nature of what occurred. Accounts of drivers jumping from burning vehicles, people escaping gun attacks, and rescues during natural disasters are just some instances of heroic rescues. I have chosen to classify these events as footprints left by those involved, as they are forever etched in historical accounts.

I find the encounter of the apostle Paul that is recorded in Acts 27 and 28 quite intriguing. This encounter occurred during the journey to Rome, and it included a snake attack which revealed the power of God. He had been taken prisoner, and prior to setting sail, he warned of treacherous times ahead. His warnings were ignored, and they had quite a tumultuous journey at sea.

On landing in Malta, following the shipwreck, the islanders built a fire to welcome them, as it was cold. In adding wood to the fire, Paul found a snake clinging to his hand as it tried to escape the heat. Acts 28:1-7 details how the islanders thought that Paul was an evil person who had just survived a shipwreck and was again being attacked. However, when Paul shook off the snake in the fire, without having any after-effects, they were all shocked. This had a riveting impact on those who witnessed it, to the point where they thought he was a magician. That encounter for those who looked on no doubt was not readily forgotten.

It is the norm for all of us to try to capture and preserve significant moments in our lives. We use videos, pictures, and anything that will record and memorialize the events. In the Bible, we read of God instructing the children of Israel to use stones as symbols of their encounters with Him and the victories they experienced during their wilderness journey. These were to serve as opportunities for testimonies of God's guidance when asked what they meant. These stones were footprints. We, too, are leaving footprints when we share our testimonies.

I have always been passionate about excellence in whatever sphere I worked. This should be of such a high caliber that whether or not I am appreciated, my work speaks. I have taught and served in various churches and educational institutions in my homeland Jamaica and overseas. For every institution that I have served, I could return there because, despite the many challenges faced, I danced well.

In one institution, one of my students received the national award for top performance in Mathematics. I have been celebrated as educator of the week and educator of the month. I have had the opportunity to lead and present in professional development workshops and have risen to the position of head of department in two subject areas and later on as a school principal. There were many firsts in the last institution that I served because of programs I implemented. In fact, I have glowing recommendations from each because I chose to work so I could leave footprints. I have a portfolio that chronicles many experiences from these different places. I have shared my story and experiences because they are footprints.

The message of dancing symbolizes for me the possibility of experiencing victory in the tough moments of life. Born out of the dream I had, there were tangible experiences that serve as my personal testimonies of victory. Those testimonies are not just a personal celebration but a witness to others that we can overcome. In sharing them, I am leaving footprints.

During the attacks, I constantly reminded myself that I had the strength within to dance despite the attacks. The Bible in Luke 10:19, tells us that we have power to trample (I say dance) on serpents ... and nothing can hurt us. This means the serpents will come but we can dance. The Message Bible describes it this way: "safe passage as you walk among snakes." Rest assured, there will be snakes along the path of life, those difficult moments, those encounters that really rock your boat.

We get various types of messages in different ways: sermons, text messages, voice notes, devotional readings. Sometimes we overlook them because they appear simplistic. I challenge us to be careful that we do not miss the messages that are sent to direct us through our struggles or the challenging seasons of our lives. Who wants to dream about snakes? Who wants to be dancing among snakes? No volunteers am sure!

There are so many popular stories that indicate that revenge or getting back at people is not deemed as healthy. The struggle to seek revenge or get even is a reality we all can identify with in various ways, whether personal or by observation. It takes maturity to take the high road when we know we have been wronged. When you find yourself in a leadership position, there is a greater demand placed on you to handle all matters professionally and ethically. Mind you, it does not guarantee that your decisions will be necessarily accepted. It is such a thorny web that is why Ghandi gave wise counsel in saying, "An eye for an eye makes the whole world blind." Be mindful of the popular statement: "Unforgiveness is like drinking poison and expecting someone else to die."

Let us face the reality that it is not always easy to go through difficult times in our lives with a smile on our faces. Our emotions go through turbulence and upheavals like any category five hurricane. There are also those seasons when we experience the eye of the storm. There were times when I grumbled, complained, and was angry, but I never lived there. I realized I had to make a choice to rise above the emotions that would destroy me and find a way to draw on God's power to go on and still serve well. I had to live out what I believed that God would vindicate me. Despite the tears and the pain, I had to let go and forgive. This for me, was how I experienced victory. I chose to look away from seeking revenge, and this was how I danced.

The Bible is replete with examples of how we should relate to each other. Many of these have even influenced popular phrases and life mantras. Do not be overcome by evil but overcome evil with good (Romans 12:21). Love your neighbor as yourself (James 2:8). Love your enemy and pray for those who persecute you (St Matthew 5:44). Do not repay anyone evil for evil (I Peter 3:9). The most challenging biblical command to us is that if your enemy is hungry, feed him, if he is thirsty give him something to drink (Romans 12:20).

If we can apply these principles, we will leave footprints when we dance. My dance symbolizes victory and I aim to dance through my day-to-day actions. This is what remains as testimonies to those whom I moved amongst. As you face your "snake fields," ask yourself: Despite all I am going through, have I been able to:

- forgive?
- find an outlet to process my thoughts?

- avoid actions/speech that reflect getting even?
- Perform my responsibilities to the best of my ability despite knowing that there are those who are undermining or slandering me?
- Find strength through prayer/counseling?

Our stories may differ, and the resolutions to our battles may seem absent or may not even have come to light. The apology may never have been written or said. Our offenders may still walk among us and look in our faces with a smile. They may even continue the same attacks on other people. Despite all this, we only have control over our own actions. The healthy challenge is to protect ourselves mentally, emotionally, physically, and spiritually. Japanese writer Harauki Murakami describes this aptly when he says:

And once the storm is over, you won't remember how you made it through, how you managed to survive. You won't even be sure whether the storm is really over. But one thing is certain. When you come out of the storm, you won't be the same person who walked in (Kafka on the Shore, www.goodreads.com).

I had a dream. I lived the dream. I encountered the snakes, yet I danced. You, too, can dance.

I *am still dancing.*

Your Gift

You have made it to the end of the book. Thank you for sticking with me! I have a gift for you. It is a devotional ebook titled, "**Dancing into Your Day: A 7-Day Devotional to Help You Begin Each Day with Renewed Hope.**" Download of copy of this **free** e-book at https://bit.ly/Dancingintoyourday.

Book Reviews

If you enjoyed this book and were impacted, tell a friend, and please write an honest review wherever you bought it online. Book reviews are the lifeblood of authors. It is social proof. Thank you.

About the Author

 **Daphne Ellis** is an educator and trained counselor who has worked in various capacities in her homeland, Jamaica and overseas. She is specialist trained in both Mathematics and English and has served as Department Head and School Principal in a few schools. Daphne is passionate about seeing people overcome difficulties and describes her work with drug addicts as one of the most interesting seasons of her life. She enjoys motivational speaking, music, writing and conducting educational workshops.

Acknowledgements

One of my favorite verses of Scripture is Ecclesiastes 3:11 which says, "God makes things beautiful in His time." This book is indeed God's timing as it became not only a means of catharsis after a difficult season, but also a legacy, marking the end of an experience at a point of major transition. I have many people, too many to mention, to whom I say a heartfelt thanks for being part of my journey over the years. Those who encouraged me to write, and did so repeatedly, those who listened to my pain, over and over, you gave me the strength to dance, and this is my gift to you.

For inspiration through her coaching, I am indebted to C. Ruth Taylor. I cannot forget the exhilaration you displayed when the title of the book was decided. You held my hand and guided me through uncharted seas. Clavia, thanks for tolerating my critique and allowing inspiration to flow as you gave me the perfect illustration for the cover, and this received a resounding approval from all who saw it.

Reverend Clinton Chisholm, I say a big thank you for helping with the editing along with inputs from Dianne Chambers, Imogene Samms, and Jean Blake.

To my sister Una, you are my main cheerleader. You know so much and always wanted the best for me, ever challenging me to aim higher.

For my dear friends from College, Donna Harrison, Jacqueline and Yvonne, you celebrated this milestone with unforgettable joy, and it meant so much. I cannot forget my High school, WCA-Class of 2022. We fought many battles, but we still danced.

References

Arnold, Amanda. (2020, April 28). The Cut, Dreams. What Does It Mean If You're Having Dreams About Snakes?
https://www.thecut.com/amp/article/dreams-about-snakes.html

Goodreads. (n.d.). Retrieved May 10, 2019. Rumi Quotes. https://www.goodreads.com/quotes/tag/rumi?page=9

Goodreads. (n.d). Retrieved May 10, 2019. The Book of Rites Quotes.
https://www.goodreads.com/work/quotes/41422067-the-book-of-rites

Jakes, T. D. (2022 January 30). Road Rage Sermon. T.D. Jakes.https://www.youtube.com/watch?v=sHIqDzKinfY

Murakami. Harauki. (n.d). Retrieved May 10, 2019.
Kafka on the Shore. www.goodreads.com.

Pass it On. (n.d). Retrieved May 10, 2019. Quotes.
https://www.quotes.pub/q/you-may-
encounter-many-defeats-but-you-must-not-be-
defeated--146369

Rádlová, S. et. al. (2019, May 9). Snakes Represent
Emotionally Salient Stimuli That May Evoke Both
Fear and Disgust. *Frontiers in Psychology*.
https://www.frontiersin.org/articles/10.3389/fp
syg.2019.01085/full

Word to di Wise. (2022, January 10). Wise Jamaican
Proverbs: A Smart Slice of Jamaican Life
https://wisejamaican.com/crab-sey-im-nuh-
trust-nuh-shadder-after-dark/

Made in the USA
Monee, IL
01 May 2022

95706587R00073